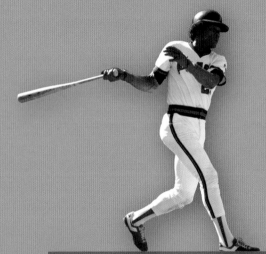

Published by Creative Education
P.O. Box 227, Mankato, Minnesota 56002
Creative Education is an imprint of The Creative Company

Design and production by Blue Design
Printed in the United States of America

Photographs by Getty Images (Jack Albin, Brian Bahr, Doug Benc, P Brouillet, Ralph Crane//Time Life Pictures, Diamond Images, Jonathan Daniel, John Dominis//Time Life Pictures, Stephen Dunn, Focus on Sport, Otto Greule Jr, JEFF HAYNES/AFP, Scott Halleran, Harry How, Jed Jacobsohn, Bill Livingston/MLB Photos, V.J. Lovero, Jim McIsaac, Christian Petersen, Rich Pilling/MLB Photos, Mike Powell, Louis Requena/MLB Photos), National Baseball Hall of Fame Library, Cooperstown, N.Y.

Library of Congress Cataloging-in-Publication Data

Gilbert, Sara.
The story of the Los Angeles Angels of Anaheim / by Sara Gilbert.
p. cm. — (Baseball: the great American game)
Includes index.
ISBN-13: 978-1-58341-477-4
1. Los Angeles Angels of Anaheim (Baseball team)—History—Juvenile literature. I. Title.
II. Series.

GV875.L6G55 2007
796.357'640979496—dc22   2006027452

First Edition
9 8 7 6 5 4 3 2 1

Cover: Outfielder Vladimir Guerrero
Page 1: First baseman Rod Carew
Page 3: Pitcher Bartolo Colon

THE STORY OF THE
LOS ANGELES ANGELS
OF ANAHEIM

by Sara Gilbert

THE STORY OF THE
Los Angeles Angels

I t's the bottom of the eighth inning, and the Angels are down 5–4 in Game 6 of the 2002 World Series. Utility man Chone Figgins starts to lead off of third, and right fielder Garret Anderson hops away from second as third baseman Troy Glaus steps to the plate against San Francisco Giants pitcher Robb Nen. Hundreds of stuffed "rally monkeys" bob in the stands of Angel Stadium as an electronic monkey dances across the scoreboard, willing the team to come from behind just once more. And just once more, the magic works: Glaus connects with the pitch and drives a double deep into the gap in left-center field, sending both Figgins and Anderson across the plate. Propelled by that timely hit, the Angels win both that game and, one night later, the World Series—their first world championship in a history spanning 42 years.

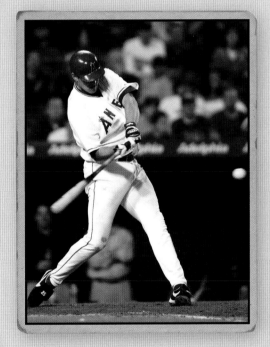

HOME OF THE HALOS

The Southern California sun hangs high over Anaheim, a suburban city on the southeastern side of Los Angeles. Its brilliance helps attract visitors to such popular destinations as Disneyland, Universal Studios, and Knotts Berry Farm. It also warms the thousands of fans who fill Angel Stadium of Anaheim, home to the city's Major League Baseball team, the Los Angeles Angels of Anaheim, for the past four decades.

The original Angels began their existence in Los Angeles in 1961, when Gene Autry, a Hollywood actor best known for his roles as a singing cowboy, was awarded an American League (AL) expansion team. With a roster that included veterans such as first baseman Ted Kluszewski and pitcher Eli Grba and rookies such as shortstop Jim Fregosi, the Los Angeles Angels cobbled together a 70–91 record that first year, setting a major-league record for the best winning percentage by a first-year team. The next year was even better, as the Angels finished only 10 games away from a playoff spot.

As the '60s went on, the Angels' success increased, fueled in part by the lively fastball of pitcher Dean Chance. In 1964, Chance was the victor in 20

The expansion "Halos" played their first nine seasons with colorful manager Bill Rigney (right) at the helm.

BILL RIGNEY

of the team's 82 wins, a feat that earned him the AL Cy Young Award at the age of 23—making him the youngest player ever to be honored as the league's best pitcher. That same year, Fregosi hit his stride. The 22-year-old shortstop batted .277 with 18 homers and 72 runs batted in (RBI) and made the first of his six appearances in the All-Star Game. Thanks to these efforts, the Angels posted their second winning record.

In 1966, the Angels moved out of Los Angeles and into Anaheim, where

ANAHEIM STADIUM – The Angels have played in Anaheim Stadium (since renamed Edison International Field and currently called Angel Stadium of Anaheim) since 1966. Renovations over the years have varied its seating capacity from 33,000 to 64,000.

A HEAVENLY START

On April 11, 1961, the Los Angeles Angels took on the Baltimore Orioles at Wrigley Field in South Central Los Angeles in their first regular-season game. As 37,352 fans watched, Detroit Tigers legend Ty Cobb threw out the first pitch—but the rest of the game was all about the Angels. Behind the complete-game pitching effort of Eli Grba and a pair of home runs by first baseman Ted Kluszewski, the Angels topped the Orioles 7–2. Although the team lost the next eight games, the mixture of experienced veterans and talented rookies worked together to compile a respectable first season under manager Bill Rigney. Grba won 11 games, and left fielder Leon Wagner led the team with 28 home runs as the Angels fought their way to a 70–91 record. Although they were almost 39 games behind the league-leading New York Yankees at the end of the season and drew the lowest attendance of all 10 AL teams, the original Los Angeles Angels were good enough to set at least one record. The team's winning percentage of .435 remains the best ever for a first-year expansion team.

ANGELS

[9]

PITCHER · NOLAN RYAN

On August 20, 1974, Angels pitcher Nolan Ryan landed in the Guinness Book of World Records when his fastball was clocked at 100.9 miles per hour. That blazing pitch was already the infamous calling card of "The Ryan Express," who tossed the first four of his seven career no-hitters with the Angels. Ryan went on to intimidate big-league batters for 27 seasons, striking out an incredible 1,176 different players on his way to setting several records—including 5,714 total "K's," the all-time major-league record. Ryan was elected to the Baseball Hall of Fame in his first year of eligibility.

STATS

Angels seasons: 1972–79

Height: 6-2

Weight: 195

- **5,714 career strikeouts**

- **7 career no-hitters**

- **8-time All-Star**

- **Baseball Hall of Fame inductee (1999)**

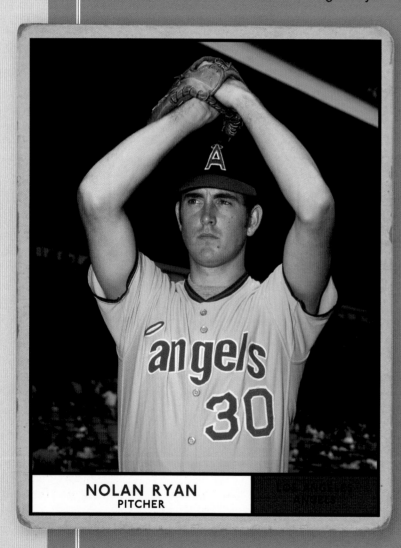

NOLAN RYAN
PITCHER

they christened the brand-new Anaheim Stadium with an exhibition game against the San Francisco Giants on April 9. With a new park and a new name—the team was now known as the California Angels—the team's fan base multiplied. Attendance jumped from 566,727 in 1965 to 1,400,321 in 1966. The new stadium also had a measurable effect on manager Bill Rigney. "The first chill I ever received in this game came when I walked into the Polo Grounds [in New York] for the first time. I received another when I walked into this park," Rigney said.

The team posted an 80–82 record that year and improved to 84–77 in 1967. Still, the Angels remained far from postseason contention. In 1968, they finished 36 games behind the league-leading Detroit Tigers, and in 1969, they ended 26 games out. The 1970 Angels played much better as a whole, and left fielder Alex Johnson laid claim to the first batting title in team history with a .329 average. He barely edged out Boston Red Sox slugger Carl Yastrzemski by getting two hits on the last day of the season. "This is my biggest individual achievement," said Johnson. "The silver bat will be an elegant addition to my trophy case."

SOME STAR POWER

**M**eanwhile, the Angels' trophy case was still bare. In an effort to start filling it, in 1972, the team traded fan favorite Jim Fregosi to the New York Mets for a young pitcher with a wild arm and a wicked fastball: Nolan Ryan. Although the Angels' coaching staff had no intention of tampering with Ryan's notorious 100-mile-per-hour pitch, they immediately set about helping control his powerful arm by having him use a more compact motion on the mound. The next year, Ryan struck out 383 batters and threw the first two of his seven career no-hitters. "I honestly never felt I was the type of pitcher to pitch a no-hitter," Ryan said after the first, on May 15, 1973, against the Kansas City Royals. Two months later, he tossed his second on July 15 in Detroit against the Tigers. "This was definitely a bigger thrill," Ryan said. "I had better stuff today, and I knew what a no-hitter meant. I probably had as good of stuff today as I've had all year."

Despite Ryan's dominance, the Angels struggled to get above .500 in the early 1970s. It wasn't until 1978 that they posted a winning record, finishing in a tie for second in the AL Western Division (the league had been split into two divisions in 1969). Still, almost two decades into their existence, the An-

NOLAN RYAN

Throwing with a velocity that often left his fingers blistered, Nolan Ryan averaged 17 wins a season for the Angels.

CATCHER · BUCK RODGERS

Buck Rodgers was just 23 when he played his first game for the Los Angeles Angels in 1961. He spent the next nine years crouching behind the plate in an Angels uniform, compiling a near-perfect .988 fielding average. Rodgers went on to serve as skipper for the Milwaukee Brewers, Montreal Expos, and California Angels, putting together a career record of 784–774. In 1992, he missed almost 90 games after being injured when the Angels' bus was involved in an accident, and his injuries had a lasting and detrimental effect on his ability to lead, causing him to be fired in May 1994.

BUCK RODGERS
CATCHER

STATS

Angels seasons: 1961–69 (1991–94 as manager)

Height: 6-2

Weight: 195

- .232 career BA

- 31 career HR

- .988 career fielding average

- 4,750 career putouts

gels had yet to experience postseason play.

That finally changed in 1979, when former star Jim Fregosi started his first full season as team manager. The Angels led the AL in runs scored (866) on their way to an 88–74 record and first-ever AL West championship. Veterans such as first baseman Rod Carew, second baseman Bobby Grich, and right fielder Dan Ford each had fine seasons, and Ryan won 16 games (including 5 shutouts), but it was stocky slugger Don Baylor who had the most spectacular season. The Angels' left fielder finished with a .296 average, 36 home runs, and a league-leading 139 RBI—numbers that earned him the AL Most

ROD CAREW – Carew was one of the best all-around hitters in baseball history, a masterful bunter and "slap hitter" with a knack for getting on base. He spent his best seasons with the Minnesota Twins but helped the Angels win two AL West titles.

Valuable Player (MVP) award. "Every day I went to the park, I knew I'd get two or three hits and some RBI," Baylor explained. "I got off to a good start and was in the right frame of mind."

The Angels squared off against the Eastern Division champion Baltimore Orioles in the AL Championship Series (ALCS). During each of the first three games, California took an early lead. But an extra-inning home run by Orioles pinch hitter John Lowenstein ended Game 1 in Baltimore's favor, and Game 2 again went to the Orioles. The Angels got their only win of the series in Game 3 before being blanked 8–0 by Baltimore in Game 4.

That first taste of postseason play whetted the Angels' appetite for more. But Ryan, a free agent after the 1979 season, jumped at the chance to return to his home state of Texas and play for the Houston Astros. Without the star hurler, the team stumbled. Baylor's offensive production was hampered by injuries, and although the sweet-swinging Carew hit his way to a .331 batting average, the 1980 Angels finished a disappointing 65–95. The strike-shortened 1981 season was only slightly more successful. After finishing at or near the bottom of the division for two consecutive seasons, it seemed there was nowhere for the Angels to go but up.

FIRST BASEMAN · WALLY JOYNER

Wally Joyner took over first base for the Angels in 1986 and promptly became a favorite among California fans, whose votes earned him a starting spot in the All-Star Game as a rookie. A year later, Joyner slammed 34 home runs and earned team MVP honors. He went on to hit more than 200 homers during his illustrious career, which spanned 16 years and four teams. Joyner returned to the Angels for his final big-league season in 2001. A religious man, Joyner today appears in movies marketed to members of The Church of Jesus Christ of Latter-Day Saints.

STATS

Angels seasons: 1986–91, 2001

Height: 6-2

Weight: 203

- **204 career HR**
- **1,106 career RBI**
- **.289 career BA**
- **1986 All-Star**

WALLY JOYNER
FIRST BASEMAN

LOS ANGELES
ANGELS

DON BAYLOR

POWER PLAY

he 1982 Angels team was, as second baseman Bobby Grich put it, "made up of veterans with sore muscles, with tired arms, with drained emotions." But those sore, tired players were supplemented by another aging veteran with a little life left in his arms: Reggie Jackson, a power-hitting right fielder who had been slamming balls out of stadiums around the league since 1967. Although he joined the Angels in the twilight of his career, he still had enough strength left to hit a league-leading 39 home runs in 1982.

With Jackson in the lineup, Baylor healthy again, and catcher Brian Downing blossoming into an offensive force of his own, the Angels racked up 93 wins and found themselves back in the ALCS. This time they faced the Milwaukee Brewers. California charged into the series, winning the first game on the strength of pitcher Tommy John's seven-hit, complete-game effort and Baylor's five RBI. When the Angels won Game 2 to take a two-games-to-none lead over the Brewers, it looked like the "Halos" were on their way to the World Series.

Then the series shifted to Milwaukee's County Stadium, where Califor-

Don Baylor was famously tough, hitting 338 career home runs and getting plunked by a pitch 267 times.

REGGIE JACKSON

A brash personality and prolific slugger, Reggie Jackson was one of baseball's top stars in the 1970s and '80s.

SECOND BASEMAN · BOBBY GRICH

Although he started his career as a shortstop, Bobby Grich made his name as a second baseman. Twice, the lanky infielder set single-season records for fielding—including when he finished the 1985 season with just two errors and a .997 fielding percentage. The most memorable of Grich's 224 home runs was his last: He hit a two-run dinger in the sixth inning of Game 5 of the 1986 ALCS that helped send the game into extra innings. But the Boston Red Sox came back to win that game, as well as the next two. Grich retired moments after the series ended.

STATS

Angels seasons: 1977–86

Height: 6-2

Weight: 190

- **6-time All-Star**
- **4-time Gold Glove winner**
- **224 career HR**
- **864 career RBI**

BOBBY GRICH
SECOND BASEMAN

LOS ANGELES
ANGELS

nia's luck changed. The Brewers won Games 3 and 4, forcing a deciding Game 5 in Milwaukee. With the Angels up 3–2 in the seventh inning, Brewers first baseman Cecil Cooper drove in two runs with a base hit. The Angels couldn't come back, losing the game and the series. Still, Angels center fielder Fred Lynn, who had a .611 average with one home run in the five-game series, was honored as the ALCS MVP.

The crestfallen Angels took their time recovering from the disappointment of 1982. The only major highlight of the 70-92 season that followed was Reggie Jackson's 500th career home run. In 1984, 15-game winner Mike Witt threw a perfect game and helped the team finish only three games out of the AL West lead. In 1985, the Angels were contenders up to the end, with four players pounding 20 or more home runs—third baseman Doug DeCinces (20), catcher Brian Downing (20), designated hitter Ruppert Jones (21), and right fielder Reggie Jackson (27). Although they faded in September, it seemed the Angels, under manager Gene Mauch, were on the rise.

California had high hopes going into the 1986 season. It had, after all, finished 1985 just one game out of the lead in the AL West. So when Grich drove the first pitch of the season out of the park, Angels fans were ready for a World Series. And the team seemed determined to give them one, produc-

BRIAN DOWNING

A fan favorite, Brian Downing often played through injuries caused by the all-out effort he gave on every play.

ROD CAREW

HAPPY HALOS

The scoreboard in Angel Stadium often flashed with three simple words in 1979: "Yes We Can." And California could. After 18 years, the Angels finally played well enough to win their division and make it to the playoffs. The leader of the charge was Don Baylor, the powerful outfielder who earned AL MVP honors after hitting .296 with 36 home runs and 139 RBI—but he had help. Second baseman Bobby Grich and right fielder Dan Ford each posted 101 RBI; Nolan Ryan earned 16 wins, one of which was one inning away from becoming his fifth no-hitter as an Angels pitcher; and

first baseman Rod Carew posted a .318 average in his first season with the team. "The biggest thing we had to overcome was that we had never won a division," said Jim Fregosi, the former star shortstop who had returned midway through the previous season as manager. "No matter how good the talent was, there seemed to be a black cloud hanging over the team. Overcoming that was special to me." Although the Angels fell to a superior Baltimore Orioles team in the playoffs, the postseason monkey was finally off their backs.

ANGELS

THIRD BASEMAN · TROY GLAUS

The Angels showed great foresight when they selected third baseman Troy Glaus in the 1997 amateur draft. The powerful young infielder got his first hit in his first game and his first home run two weeks later. He swatted almost 200 more long balls in an Angels uniform, including seven during the team's successful 2002 postseason campaign. It was Glaus's double in Game 6 of the World Series that scored the winning runs and forced a seventh game. In 2003, he became the first member of the Angels since 1986 to be voted into the starting lineup of the All-Star Game.

TROY GLAUS
THIRD BASEMAN

LOS ANGELES ANGELS

STATS

Angels seasons: 1998–2004

Height: 6-5

Weight: 240

• **4-time All-Star**

• **2002 World Series MVP**

• **716 career RBI**

• **257 career HR**

ing 25 come-from-behind victories at Angel Stadium for a division-winning 92–70 mark. Pitcher Don Sutton earned his 300th career victory in June, and young first baseman Wally Joyner had an incredible season, batting .290 and driving in 100 runs. Even an aging Reggie Jackson proved he could still muscle the ball out of the park, belting three home runs in one game.

The Angels met the Boston Red Sox in the ALCS and dominated three of the first four games. It looked as if they had the series locked up in Game 5, when they entered the ninth inning with a 5–2 lead. Unfortunately, former Angels star Don Baylor then hit a two-run homer for Boston. Then, with a man on base and two strikes against him, Red Sox outfielder Dave Henderson sent a ball high over the wall. Boston went on to win the 7–6 game in 11 innings and took the next two games as well, moving on to the World Series as the Angels went home brokenhearted. As they flew back after the final game, owner Gene Autry addressed his players with the best movie-star smile he could muster. "Look, you did your best," he told the players. "Your best on this day wasn't good enough."

LONG BALLS AND LITTLE BALL

The 1982 Angels featured one of the best home run hitters of all time: Reggie Jackson, who already had 425 homers under his belt when he signed with California before the season began. Apart from the boisterous slugger, Gene Mauch's Angels also had some of the best team players in the league, a solid core of unselfish hitters who helped coin the term "little ball." Between Jackson's league- and team-leading 39 home runs, Brian Downing's 175 hits, and the rest of the team's 114 sacrifice bunts, the 1982 Angels scored 814 runs and won 93 games. But even though they had amassed such an amazing record, the Angels had to defeat the Texas Rangers in the second-to-last game of the season in order to steal a playoff berth away from the Kansas City Royals. With their 6–4 victory, the Angels earned only their second appearance in postseason play. Despite jumping out to a two-game lead over the Milwaukee Brewers in the ALCS, the Angels stumbled when the games shifted to the Brewers' home turf, losing all three of the final games. Still, the team's long-ball hits and little-ball techniques helped California post its best record ever—until the stellar play of its 2002 world-championship season.

REGGIE JACKSON

FALLING STARS

I t would be a long time before the Angels would see the post-season again. For the rest of the 1980s and into the '90s, the team spiraled downward. Even offensive spark plug Wally Joyner, a first baseman who hit 34 home runs in 1987, and wiry pitching ace Chuck Finley, who recorded 18 wins in both 1990 and 1991, couldn't get the team back to the playoffs.

After suffering losing seasons in both 1987 and 1988, the 1989 Angels won

WALLY JOYNER – Joyner was an early bloomer, becoming the ninth player ever to drive in more than 100 runs in each of his first two big-league seasons (1986 and 1987). Although his career lasted 14 years after that, he never managed 100 RBI in a season again.

ANGELS

91 games. Newly acquired pitcher Bert Blyleven led the team with 17 wins, just ahead of Finley's 16 victories. Another star was reliever Bryan Harvey, who picked up 25 saves for the Angels. Although these pitching efforts kept California in contention for most of the season, a six-game losing streak in late September stalled the Angels' momentum and knocked them out of the postseason chase.

The Angels hung close to the .500 mark in the early 1990s but still found themselves well out of the playoff race for the first few seasons of the decade. Then, buoyed by the bats of shortstop Gary DiSarcina, right fielder Tim Salmon, and center fielder Jim Edmonds, they battled back into contention during a strike-shortened 1994 season. The team seemed poised to make a move up the standings soon.

That move came in 1995. California got off to a swift start, compiling 20 wins by the end of May, winning 14 more in June, and maintaining a winning record throughout the season. Edmonds and Salmon were assisted by rookie right fielder Garret Anderson, who won AL Player of the Month honors with a .410 batting average in July. By the time August rolled around, the Angels had a commanding 11-game lead in the AL West.

Then came one of the most memorable collapses in team history. California ended August with a nine-game losing streak and repeated that woeful feat in the middle of September. When the regular season came to an end on

SHORTSTOP · JIM FREGOSI

Jim Fregosi joined the Los Angeles Angels as a 19-year-old in 1961 and became the team's first star. The power-hitting shortstop compiled more than 1,400 hits and hit for the cycle (getting a single, double, triple, and homer in the same game) twice during his time in California. Although he was traded to the New York Mets for pitcher Nolan Ryan in 1971, he returned as a manager in 1978 and led the Angels to their first division title. He left the Angels' staff in 1981, but Fregosi's managerial career continued until 2000, when he won his 1,000th game with the Toronto Blue Jays.

JIM FREGOSI
SHORTSTOP

STATS

Angels seasons: 1961–71 (1978–81 as manager)

Height: 6-1

Weight: 190

- **6-time All-Star**

- **1,726 career hits**

- **706 career RBI**

- **Uniform number (11) retired by Angels**

Veteran curveball expert Bert Blyleven
tossed an AL-best five shutouts in
1989, his last great season.

BERT BLYLEVEN

LEFT FIELDER · BRIAN DOWNING

Nobody worked harder than Brian Downing. In an era when ballplayers rarely lifted weights, Downing pumped enough iron to transform himself from a scrawny catcher to an All-Star slugger and near-perfect fielder. In 1978, he set a team record for catchers with a .993 fielding percentage; then, between 1981 and 1983, after he had moved to the outfield, he set an AL record with a streak of 244 errorless games. His remarkable streak included 330 errorless chances in 1982, also an AL record. That feat helped earn him a place on the Angels' All-Time team, as selected by then-owner Gene Autry in 1986.

STATS

Angels seasons: 1978–90

Height: 5-10

Weight: 194

• .267 career BA

• 275 career HR

• 2,099 career hits

• 1,073 career RBI

BRIAN DOWNING
LEFT FIELDER

October 1, California had lost its lead and was tied for first place with the Seattle Mariners, forcing a one-game playoff to decide the AL West winner. An incredible pitching performance by ace Randy Johnson gave the Mariners the win and squashed the Angels' postseason hopes. "We were the best team for three months," DiSarcina said. "But you've got to be the best team when it counts. Granted, we've had injuries, but so have other teams. The real good teams overcome it; they're capable of turning it up at crunch time. We haven't done it, plain and simple. We've lost that intimidation, that edge, the feeling that we're going to go out and hammer teams."

To sharpen their edge, the Angels tried a series of changes during the next few years. First, they brought up speedy first baseman Darin Erstad, who stole 23 bases and scored 99 runs in 1997. Then they replaced manager Marcel Lachemann with Terry Collins, changed their name to the Anaheim Angels, and, in 1998, moved into their newly remodeled home stadium, now known as Angel Stadium of Anaheim. As their roster of young players matured and the pitching staff flourished behind the dominance of intimidating save artist Troy Percival, the Angels started to pick up speed as the century came to a close.

EARNING THEIR WINGS

he Angels' new century started with a new manager: Mike Scioscia, a longtime catcher with the Los Angeles Dodgers who had ended his playing career in 1994. Scioscia led the Angels to a winning record in 2000. Young third baseman Troy Glaus, who had joined the team as a shy 21-year-old in 1998, had developed into a bona fide power hitter by this time, leading the league with 47 home runs in 2000 and hitting 41 more in 2001. "He's capable of hitting .300 with 40 home runs and a ton of walks and playing the best third base in the league, if not all of baseball," said Angels bench coach Joe Maddon.

With Glaus's help, the Angels were soon to become the best team in baseball—but first they would have to endure the worst start in team history. On April 23, 2002, their record was 6–14, leaving them more than 10 games behind Seattle in the division standings. Then, shortstop David Eckstein hit grand slams in consecutive games, and the team pounded the Indians 21–2 in Cleveland. Suddenly, the Angels had a new spark. By the end of May, they had improved to 30–21. By the end of June, the Angels were only three and a half games out of the lead in the AL West.

MONKEY BUSINESS

It might have been Troy Glaus's power, Garret Anderson's consistency, or Troy Percival's late-inning dominance. Or it might have been the miracle of the monkey that propelled the Anaheim Angels to a world championship in 2002. The Rally Monkey made its first appearance on June 6, when the Angels were losing to the San Francisco Giants. The Angel Stadium video crew attempted to rouse the crowd with a clip of a dancing monkey from the movie *Ace Ventura, Pet Detective*. Not only did the fans respond, but the team did too: in the ninth inning, the Angels scored two runs to win the game. As that clip continued to charm the team, the Angels decided to hire a monkey of their own: Katie, a white-faced capuchin monkey who had already garnered attention for her role in the television sitcom *Friends*. Katie became the star of a series of Rally Monkey film clips, including the popular "Jump Around" and "Believe in the Power of the Rally Monkey." She also became one of the stars of the season, having her most potent effect in Game 6 of the World Series between the Angels and Giants, when she helped the team rally in the seventh and eighth innings to force a series-clinching Game 7.

CENTER FIELDER · DARIN ERSTAD

A former punter for the University of Nebraska football team, Darin Erstad was selected by the Angels with the first overall pick of the 1995 amateur draft. He quickly became a star, batting .299 in his first full season and climbing to .355 in the Angels' 2002 world championship season. His strength at the plate was matched by his hustle in the field.

DARIN ERSTAD
CENTER FIELDER

LOS ANGELES
ANGELS

Erstad played near-perfect defense in both the outfield and infield, earning Gold Glove awards for his performances in center field and at first base—becoming the first major-leaguer to receive the award for both positions.

STATS

Angels seasons: 1996–present

Height: 6-2

Weight: 210

- **2-time All-Star**

- **3-time Gold Glove winner**

- **2000 AL leader in singles (170)**

- **.286 career BA**

As the season progressed, Anaheim and the Oakland A's fought for the top spot in the division. With outstanding pitching by Jarrod Washburn and rookie reliever Brendan Donnelly, the Angels seemed destined to overtake the A's. But then Oakland got hot, winning 20 consecutive games and ultimately winning the AL West. Anaheim finished four games behind Oakland, but its 99–63 record was good enough to win the AL Wild Card, sending the Angels to the postseason for the first time in 16 years.

The Angels and another rookie reliever, Francisco Rodriguez, a September call-up from the team's minor-league system, caught fire in the playoffs. Anaheim quickly dispatched of the New York Yankees in the AL Division Series (ALDS), then moved on to face the Minnesota Twins in the AL Championship Series (ALCS). Up three games to one by Game 5, the Angels put on an impressive offensive display, scoring 10 runs on 10 hits in the seventh inning and sealing both a 13–5 victory and a trip to the 2002 World Series.

The Angels faced the San Francisco Giants and star slugger Barry Bonds in an all-California World Series that went a nail-biting seven games. With the series on the line and the Angels trailing in Game 6, Glaus ripped a double that brought home both the tying and winning runs and forced a deciding Game 7. The next night, Garret Anderson's third-inning, three-run double helped topple the Giants 4–1. After 42 frustrating years, the Angels had finally won a World Series. "These fans have been waiting a long, long time for

BRENDAN DONNELLY – Donnelly made his big-league debut in 2002 at the age of 30 after having spent 10 years in the minors. He capitalized on his opportunity, earning All-Star status in 2003, a rare accomplishment for a set-up (non-closer) relief pitcher.

RIGHT FIELDER • GARRET ANDERSON

Garret Anderson weighed 190 pounds when he joined the Angels as a 22-year-old rookie in 1994. During the next decade, Anderson not only filled out his frame but his statistics as well. Always known for his ability to hit for average (he holds the Angels team record for most career hits), he also developed into a feared power hitter, belting 35 home runs in 2000 and compiling 241 round-trippers through 2006. Despite his success, Anderson remained under the radar of most baseball fans nationwide until he and the Angels caught fire during the 2002 playoffs.

GARRET ANDERSON
RIGHT FIELDER

LOS ANGELES
ANGELS

STATS

Angels seasons: 1994–present

Height: 6-3

Weight: 225

- **3-time All-Star**

- **2-time AL leader in doubles**

- **241 career HR**

- **2,081 career hits**

WHAT'S IN A NAME?

Since their inception in 1961, the Angels have been known by a number of different official names. Originally, when they played in Wrigley Field and Dodger Stadium, both in Los Angeles, they were the Los Angeles Angels. Then, when they moved to the suburb of Anaheim in 1965, they became known more broadly as the California Angels. And when that same stadium was completely remodeled prior to the 1996 season, they once again changed names—this time to the Anaheim Angels. But the biggest change came in January 2005, when the team's ownership announced another new name: the Los Angeles Angels of Anaheim. Team executives said the change would help them market the team to the entire Southern California region, while still complying with the provision in the team's lease with Angel Stadium that "Anaheim" be included in the team's name. Unfortunately, the new name spurred a legal dispute between the team's owners and the city of Anaheim, which believed that the change violated the "spirit of the lease." No matter which side wins the legal battle, which remained unsettled as of early 2007, the Angels will always be the "Halos" to those who love them best.

this," Glaus said as he accepted his series MVP trophy. "And I know we're happy to be part of the team to bring it to them."

The Angels slumped to 77–85 in 2003, but they returned to form in the years that followed, assembling three winning seasons and capturing the AL West crown in 2004 and 2005. Powering the team were such newcomers as right fielder Vladimir Guerrero, a dangerous slugger, and big pitcher Bartolo Colón, who won the 2005 Cy Young Award with a 21–8 record. But the Angels could not reach the World Series, falling to the eventual world champions in the playoffs both seasons—the Boston Red Sox in the 2004 ALDS and the Chicago White Sox in the 2005 ALCS.

Those postseason defeats left the Halos hungry for more, and with talents such as flamethrowing closer Francisco Rodriguez and newly signed outfielder Gary Matthews Jr. in place, they believed they had the firepower to reach baseball's ultimate stage again. "We think we have the makings of a pretty good ballclub," Angels general manager Bill Stoneman said in the spring of 2007. "And we weren't all that bad last year."

With their many years of bad luck finally behind them, the Angels and their loyal fans have finally become perennial contenders in the playoffs. And as they move forward with a roster stocked with power and a pitching staff heavy on talent, there's no reason to think they won't continue to win under California's eternally bright summer sun.

Vladimir Guerrero batted .337 and bashed 39 homers in 2004 to win the first AL MVP award in team history.

VLADIMIR GUERRERO

MANAGER • MIKE SCIOSCIA

Although Mike Scioscia flirted with the idea of leaving baseball when his big-league playing career ended in 1992, the All-Star catcher couldn't break the baseball habit entirely. In 2000, he became the Angels' 16th manager and has since become the best in team history. Not only is his .537 winning percentage second to none in franchise history, but he is also the only Angels skipper with a world championship ring. In 2002, the calmly focused Scioscia led a team that faltered early in the season to a Wild Card berth in the playoffs and eventually a World Series victory against the San Francisco Giants.

STATS

Angels seasons as manager: 2000–present

Height: 6-2

Weight: 245

Managerial Record: 609–525

World Series Championship: 2002

MIKE SCIOSCIA
MANAGER

THE SINGING COWBOY

Gene Autry became famous singing songs from atop his constant companion, Champion the Wonder Horse. During his legendary career in show business, Autry wrote more than 200 songs, appeared in almost 100 movies, and produced his own TV series. By the time "the singing cowboy" retired from show business in the early 1960s, he had amassed a considerable fortune—and he decided to invest some of it in the Anaheim Angels when the team joined the AL in 1961. Autry was the sole owner of the Angels for more than 30 years and became almost as recognizable on the baseball diamond as he had been on the silver screen. It didn't hurt that he continued to wear the trademark white cowboy hat that had defined his presence in film and on TV. Autry, who sold part of the franchise to the Disney company in 1997, died at the age of 91 a year later and never got to see the team he helped build win a World Series. But when the Angels finally captured the crown in 2002, the team's longtime owner was present in spirit. As the Angels celebrated their Game 7 victory, outfielder Tim Salmon waved a white cowboy hat in the air in Autry's honor.

ANGELS

INDEX